WHO'S WHO AT THE ZOO
SWINGING ANIMAL TALES
WITH THIRTY DRAWINGS

by

Violet Gordon

DORRANCE & COMPANY

Philadelphia

Dedicated to Bonnie, David, Burt III, Bambi, Molly, Julie and Jill—who made my zoo trips so frequent and so delightful!

Animals are such agreeable
friends; they ask no questions,
they pass no criticisms.

George Eliot

CONTENTS

Page

ACKNOWLEDGEMENTS

In writing and illustrating this book I am deeply indebted to Bryant Arbuckle, of the Phoenix Zoo, for his co-operation as a consultant and to Desmond Morris for his charming comments of encouragement. Mr. Arbuckle and Mr. Morris, as well as Leonard Lee Rue III, William Bridges, Ruth Weihrich and Gordon Smith, also generously supplied animal photos which have assured authenticity for my illustrations. I wish to express my thanks for this help.

There are others I wish to acknowledge for inspiration. They have assisted directly and indirectly—my parents, who bequeathed to me an inherent love of animals, and those dear people whose glowing interest radiated a sustained light of encouragement.

Gratefully, I wish also to acknowledge the Phoenix Zoo, the Bronx Zoo, the Buffalo Zoological Society, the Zoological Society of London, the San Diego Zoo, the Paris Zoo, and all those amazing animals that contribute so much to our joie de vivre!

THE MONKEY

Cheers!
    for the monkey
       and the chimpanzee
Acrobats of high degree
Trapeze artists so fantastic
Inconceivably
       a
     n   s
   m   t
  y   i
 g   c
With spirits blithe
    and bodies lithe
      on long arms they swing
      as they do their thing

Then suddenly they pause
    for audience applause—
    O what pretenders
    are those Oscar contenders

Performing so truly great
      these exhibitionists rate
      a resounding success
      in the monkey business
So light up the neon sign
      and let
            the chimp and
                monkey shine!

1

THE OSTRICH

This bird struts
    and shuffles
In his tu tu ruffles
    of plumage that unites
    with his pale pink tights
For ballerina skits
    as he gracefully flits
    making the rounds
    in his 300 pounds

A paradox absurd
    that this nonflying bird
    is the speediest of all
For, being eight feet tall
    his legs are so long
    and his kick so strong
    to be specific
    it's a knockout terrific

And those legs of great power
    speed
        at
            thirty miles
                per hour!

THE CHEETAH

Wonderful topics—
    on this cat from the tropics
Who defies natural laws
    with permanently extended claws
Most dog-like of all
He's man's hunting animal

For speed—
    he's no stinter
    a powerful sprinter
    can go sixty miles per
    should the necessity occur
Speeding on legs long and lanky
    he's most fleet and he's swanky
    tawny coated with spots
    this cat has lots
For—
    nature
       did not cheat
          a
          Cheetah!

THE WOODCHUCK—GROUNDHOG OR MARMOT

This little fat friend
        muses no end
Sitting in the sun
        in complete oblivion
With snout to the skies
        he looks so wise

        Eyes blink
                as he appears to think
        Nose twitches
                at the air's fragrant riches
                of a blossom's scent
                he smiles content
                with the flutter of birds,
        But without any words
He has the wisdom of Zen
                when
                all summer he feeds
                to supply winter needs
        For his annual date
                to go underground
                          and
                            hibernate!

THE WALLAROO

An Australian wallaroo
       is a medium sized kangaroo
The female's pouch
       like an abdominal couch
Is where her babies reside
       and stay snuggly inside
       a few months or so
       as from one inch they grow
Then peer out to see
       such strange scenery
So tiny at birth
       they soon gather girth
With big hind legs for hopping
       they go leaping and clopping
But sit—if they care
       on what seems like a chair
       it's a long thick tail
       and the prop doesn't fail—
         Lucky!
Lucky too—
       For the lady wallaroo
       that the pouch doesn't sag
       for the pouch
            is
             her
               bag!

THE GEMSBOK

The oryx gazella
        is a strange looking fella
A couple of slim horns
        scarcely adorns

"Does he wear a mask?"
        you might easily ask

So to confide—
        it is bonafide—
For the head matches
The legs black and white patches
Though the body is tan
On this African

The strange color scheme
        is like a wild dream
Yes, this antelope's odd
        because he's so mod

Without any doubt—
        just a
                psychedelic
                        drop-out!

11

THE PENGUIN

These birds are so cool
        as they move in a school
Tuxedos they wear
        with a nonchalant air

Adorable creatures
        with human-like features
        they wiggle and waddle
        and move with a toddle

In an upright walk
        struts the great auk
        erect he goes
        on little webbed toes

Into the sea he flings
        swims with his wings
And away he putters
        his feet as his rudders
For that is his plight
        a bird
            without
                flight!

THE ZEBRA

This equine animal
        appears theatrical
No horse stereotypes
        in his black and white stripes
It's protective coloration
        for zebra preservation
As lions bescour them
        and promptly devour them

One has to defer
        to his bad temper
It defies domestication
        on any location
However, this ass
        who feeds on grass
Is really quite mild
        though thought of as wild

Could it be he is typed
        because he is striped
And associated alas—
        with
           old
              Alcatraz!

THE CAMEL

This one hump dromedary
   has a water depositary
It's a pouch in a paunch
   that keeps him so staunch
For out on the desert
   he's quite an expert
A fine beast of burden,
   devoid of allergen
He survives on scrub plants
   that the desert waste scants
He's really no chump
   has fat stored in his bump
And he's built to withstand
   the blowing of sand
With nostrils protected
   and eyes not neglected
With lashes so glamorous
   this camel
      seems
        amorous!

THE PRAIRIE DOG

This fellow's not very tall
       just twelve inches in all
       as he stands to his height
       inveigling a bite

This rodent so dear
       will at times disappear
For just a brief furlough
       he takes to his burrow
For he lives underground
       where his friends all abound
A gregarious breed
       —colonizing at need
These dogs of the prairie
       though cute and though chary
Are dogs—
       just you hark—
You can tell
       by
          their
             bark!

THE GIRAFFE

He's twenty feet tall
      rarely bends at all
Not even to eat
      for he's very discreet
      as from trees he retrieves
      his dinner of leaves

Though his front legs are longer
      the hind legs are stronger
A tall animal is he
      with lengthened vertebrae
His little head bumps
      are really horn stumps
Such anatomical features
      make for strange creatures

With moves so demure
      and moos so obscure
      his use no one knows
Do you suppose
      Giraffes
         are
           for
             laughs?

THE LLAMA

This animal's rated
        as domesticated
In South America, he's bred
        in the mountain's 'tis said
        below the snow line
        it suits him just fine

Now here's the imbroglio
        a descendant of the quanaco
        he's in the camel family though smaller
        and like a sheep, though taller
        to the alpaca he's related
        also, the vicuna it's stated

With such a relation
        can he find identification?

Well, this beast of burden so long
        is very gentle though strong
So —
        like a lamb
          is
            the
              llama!

THE BLACKBUCK

The female is hornless
      pale brown and adornless
      but truly germane
      for out on the plain
      she gives an alarm
           of impending harm
      bounding into the air
           so the herd is aware

Then like an explosion
      they bound into motion
      their gallop is fleet
           on small pointed feet

The buck named Black
      seems about to attack
      and plays antagonist
      though what is the twist
      are his horns so unique
           long and oblique
      they turn curlique
      they're
          really
             corkscrew!

THE WHITETAIL

Have you ever seen
　　　　anyone so serene?
In a hide most posh
　　　　of trusting camouflage—
Both the buck and the hind
　　　　are a real docile kind
For their cares are so slight
　　　　as they take off in flight
And gracefully ignore
　　　　a hungry predator.

Though the buck's antlers pierce,
　　　　and as a weapon—are fierce
The deer's real defense
　　　　is a strong extra sense
　　　　trouble to foresee
　　　　with innate ability
Like the fawns that know
　　　　to lie still, sans the doe

O, nature was benign
　　　　to create so divine
A whitetail—it's clear
　　　　the deer
　　　　　　is a
　　　　　　　　dear!

27

THE JAGUAR

It really astounds
      that he goes 300 pounds

This largest cat
      is a real plutocrat
While appearing fastidious
He's really insidious
      for he preys atrociously
      and devours ferociously

The tapirs and deer
      have plenty to fear
For this magnificent animal
      is practically cannibal

A formidable feline—
      in a coat
          too
            divine!

THE ELEPHANT

He's ten feet tall
  six tons in all
Which is tremendous
  and quite stupendous
To realize—
  for all his size
  he's a confirmed dietarian—
   strictly vegetarian

This thick skinned guy
  with the sensitive eye
Stands and stares
  sometimes he glares
Then stomps and stalks
  as on he walks
Perhaps he frets
  'cause he never forgets
And now in a jam
  he tries to remember
    who
     I
     am!

Violet Gordon

THE SHEEP

From birth
     just a lamb
Both the ewe and the ram
     guileless
     completely wileless
     no hostility
     just docility

With a baa for a bleat
They give skins, wool and meat

With gifts so numerous
Does it seem humorous
That they
     are
       sheepish
         benefactors?

THE GOAT

It's simply incredible
       the things she finds edible
Baubles and bangles
       and all sorts of spangles

Yet it's quite original
       that her milk is medicinal
       it's sweet and nourishing
       and generally flourishing

Besides,
       she yields flesh and hair
       that's unquestionably fair

So it's remarkable to note
       that this cud-chewing goat
       gives more
           than
              she
                gets!

THE LION

The long tufted tail
        distinguished the male
His heavy neck mane
        gives him his name
"The King"
        is regal indeed
        of aristocratic breed
Though a most social cat
        in his native habitat
Where he hob-nobs in a pride
        other lions at his side
            apparently idolized
This cat
        appears
           lionized!

THE BEAR

The cub
        is so coy-like
        actually, toy-like
At birth
        but a pound
        cuddly and round
He's playful and fun
But—
        becomes a half ton
Withal
        we maintain
        he can entertain
            by begging and dancing
            benignly entrancing

Despite all his charm
        we never disarm
        for all of the cuteness
        there's still great astuteness

His hugging is lecherous
Bare facts are
        he's
            treacherous!

THE OWL

The owl resembles a cat
      with a face round and flat
      but looks so wise
           with bright round eyes
              that wink
                 and blink
     as he appears to think
     in a solemn way
        and say,
              "Tu whit to who-o-o
              I'm no parvenu
              I can hoot and whistle
              and screech like a missile
              I'm a fierce little scrapper
              in my soft feather wrapper
              that muffles my flight
              in the dead of night"
So—on this nocturnal way
     he seeks living prey
Yes, he looks so wise
     but don't minimize
        this carnivorous chap—
       known as
           the great
              mouse-trap!

THE WOLF

Villain of legend and lore
      Red Riding Hood, Three Pigs and more
Depicted as the predator of the weak
      with a mean destructive streak
Now the bounty hunter's prey
      in northern countries for big pay
'Tis sad to put it most succinct
      the wolf is practically extinct
Diminished through false accusation
      he's headed for extermination

Exuberant animal of the wild
      known through myth to every child
Noble beast, intelligent one
      playful yearling, full of fun
Reared in structured family behavior
      the dominant male a family savior
Misunderstood in so many ways
      now with strictly numbered days
This magnificent dog
      soon won't be at all—
Deplorable—
      the demise
            of the old
                  wolf call!

THE SITATUNGA

"Marsh Buck"
            is the name
Waterways
            the game
For rather than romp
            he'll sit in a swamp
The water he prefers
            for general traverse
            And swims very well
            great distances tell
Sometimes underwater
            like a dread-naughter
            In the water he'll rest
            just head above the crest
With horns rising two feet
            On this water athlete
            And during that session
            he gives the impression
            that this antelope's
                        got
                              two
                                    periscopes!

45

THE WHITE RHINO

By gad—
       he looks sad—
An enormous land mammal
With humps unlike a camel—
For—
       besides a back hump
       he's got a nose with a bump
       surely not pretty
And what a pity—
       there's so much of him
       eight thousand pounds trim
For he feeds on scrubs
       grasses and shrubs
       from the savanna, his home
       where he freely can roam
          leisurely, apathetic
          unenergetic

Once almost extinct
He now has his precinct
       on a protected strand
          in South Zululand
Where he travels in a pair
       quite unaware
He's a really odd guy
       nature created—
          but
            why?

THE TIGER

He's the greatest cat —
   in his native habitat

The most handsome of all
   called
      "Beautiful Beast of Bengal"

In a coat so exclusive
The feline's elusive
   seldom aggressive
   with a deportment impressive
   this huge carnivore
   avoids trouble galore

   Subsists on his catches
   of whatever he snatches
   for with seldom a bungle
   he snares prey in the jungle

   Keeps himself trim
   with a most frequent swim
And wherever he goes
   it very clearly shows
That to him all defer
'Cause
  you don't
    hold
     a
     tiger!

THE OTTER

Charming fellow
       full of play
In a most delightful way
With his family he'll ride
       a mud or snow slide
And then at a whim
       he'll dive and swim
And perhaps catch a fish
       or frog or crayfish
       from an inland waterway
       in Alaska, U.S.A.
While people all dote
       on his valuable coat
Everyone will admit
       he makes a big hit
       because he's so unconforming
       —so great at performing
A joy to behold—
       and now that you're told
       you just got'er
           see
              an
                otter!

THE

COUGAR PUMA PANTHER CATAMOUNT MOUNTAIN LION

Isn't it fair game
    to ask,
        "What's in a name?"
When he has so many
    and is known by any

This lion so slick
    is a bright little trick
    for at the age of two
        he knows what to do
    he can stalk and hide
        or pounce
            for homicide

When his baby spotted pelt
    turns to a tawny felt
Then this wild cat is known
    to go it alone
Except to mate
    he makes no date

Strange
    how people think he can
        co-exist with man
He can—for being bright
    he simply
        stays
            out of
                sight!

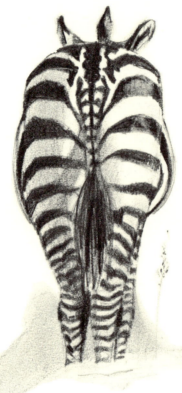

So
 it's been fun to regale
 an animal tale
 of a winsome zoo friend
Now to you—
 an adieu
For this is—

   THE END!